Art

Written by Tanya DeStefano

Art makes you think or feel . . .

or wonder about what
you see.

Sometimes it
might make
you laugh.

3

Art can be a painting.
Paintings can look real ...

or make-believe.

Not all paintings hang on walls.
Paintings can be done on a van . . .

or on the side of a building.

Art can be a statue.
Statues let you see the art
from many sides.

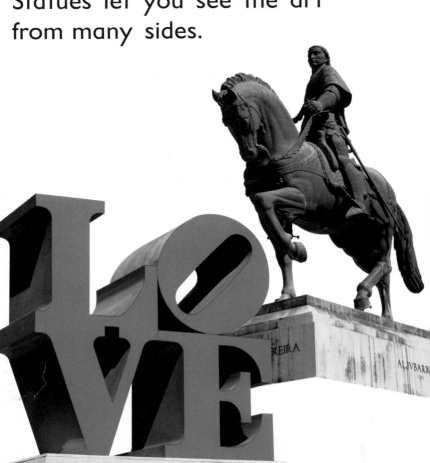

Art can be a building.
People visit some buildings just
to enjoy how they look.

Some art is for wearing.
Artists make beautiful costumes
to wear on special days.

Artists make T-shirts you
can wear every day.

Some art can fly.
Hot-air balloons make beautiful
colors part of the sky.

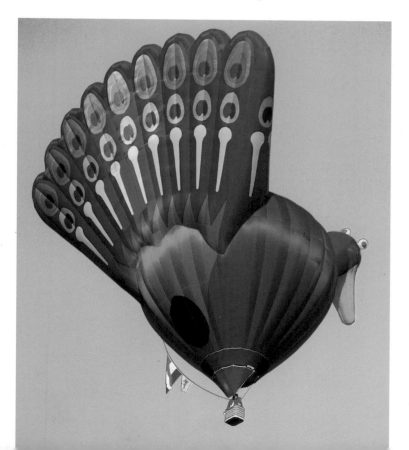

Dancers make art
by moving to music.

Music is art you can hear.

Artists make sand castles
and carve things in ice.

Their art does not last very long.

Art can be found in nature.
Flowers and sunsets can be art, too.

And some art is special just to you.